W9-DCF-016

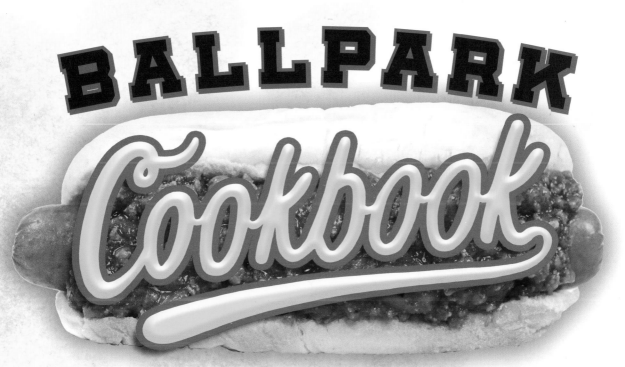

BALLPARK Cookbook

THE NATIONAL LEAGUE

RECIPES INSPIRED BY
Baseball Stadium Foods

★ BY ★

Katrina Jorgensen

CAPSTONE PRESS
a Capstone imprint

Table of Contents

Atlanta Braves Baseball Club

TURNER FIELD

LOCATION
Atlanta, Georgia
OPENED
1997
CAPACITY
49,586
NICKNAMES
The Ted

The Braves have been calling Turner Field home since 1997. Named after media mogul and team owner, Ted Turner, this stadium has helped guide the design of future ballparks. It's both baseball and fan friendly as visitors can walk around the lower concourse and still keep an eye on the game while getting something to nosh on. But the Braves' stay at the Ted, as locals call it, is about to end. Their lease is up in 2016, and a new stadium is already in the works. In 2017, the team will be playing at Sun Trust Park in Cobb County, just north of Atlanta, Georgia.

SHRIMP PO' BOY

with SWEET 'N' SPICY COLESLAW & PEACH SMOOTHIE

While at the Ted, one fan fave is the Yicketty Yamwich — inspired by Chipper Jones's slang term for a home run. This sandwich is like a grilled cheese stuffed with braised short ribs and spinach, and features a spiced apple butter. But there are many southern treats to feast on from pulled pork sandwiches to this flavorful, slaw-stuffed shrimp po' boy.

SHRIMP PO' BOY

PREP	COOK	MAKES
10	**6**	**4**
MINUTES	MINUTES	SANDWICHES

	INGREDIENTS	
◇	2 tablespoons	all-purpose flour
◇	1 teaspoon	seafood seasoning
◇	1 teaspoon	paprika
◇	½ teaspoon	salt
◇	½ teaspoon	ground black pepper
◇	½ pound	peeled, deveined,
◇		tail-off shrimp
◇	1 tablespoon	olive oil
◇	4	French sandwich rolls,
◇		split in half
◇	4 ounces	Sweet 'n' Spicy Coleslaw
◇	10–12	pickle slices

1 Mix the flour, seafood seasoning, paprika, salt, and black pepper on a plate. Dredge the shrimp to coat all sides in the mix.

2 In a skillet, heat olive oil over medium-high heat.

3 Carefully add the shrimp and cook 3 minutes on each side or until slightly browned. When done, set aside.

4 To assemble, place ¼ of the shrimp on the bottom half of the bread. Scoop ¼ cup of the coleslaw on top of the shrimp, followed by pickle slices, then the top half of the sandwich.

5 Serve immediately.

THE *PEACH* STADIUM

Georgia is well-known as the "Peach State," and Turner Field lives up to this fruity moniker. From the famous peach cobbler at 755 Club at Turner Field to locally made peach-flavored ice cream, sweet treats abound throughout the stadium. Afterward, work off calories at the kid-friendly game called the "Peach Pitch," located at the stadium's West Pavilion, where youngsters can test their skills by throwing peaches into baskets.

SWEET 'N' SPICY COLESLAW

PREP	COOK	MAKES
5 MINUTES	0 MINUTES	4 SERVINGS

INGREDIENTS		
◇	1 cup	coleslaw mix
◇	2 tablespoons	mayonnaise
◇	1 tablespoon	sour cream
◇	1 tablespoon	apple cider vinegar
◇	2 teaspoons	hot sauce
◇	1 teaspoon	honey
◇	½ teaspoon	salt

1 Combine the coleslaw mix, mayonnaise, sour cream, apple cider vinegar, hot sauce, honey, and salt in a mixing bowl. Stir well.

2 Serve on Shrimp Po' Boys. Store leftovers in an airtight container in refrigerator for up to 3 days.

PEACH SMOOTHIE

PREP	COOK	MAKES
5 MINUTES	0 MINUTES	4 SMOOTHIES

INGREDIENTS		
◇	1 cup	plain yogurt
◇	1 cup	milk
◇	2 cups	frozen peaches
◇	¼ cup	orange juice
◇	1 teaspoon	honey
◇	8	ice cubes

1 Combine all ingredients in a blender. Blend until smooth.

2 Pour into glasses for serving.

MIA

MARLINS PARK

LOCATION	
Miami, Florida	
OPENED	
2012	
CAPACITY	
36,742	

The Marlins joined the National League in 1993, making them one of the newest teams in Major League Baseball. And during their first years, they shared Sun Life Stadium with the NFL's Dolphins. While the bad weather doesn't stop a football game, it can be tough to get in nine innings with Florida's hot, humid, and rainy weather. So in 2012, the team moved into Marlins Park. It's currently the newest of all pro ballparks and features a retractable roof. It's a nice and cozy stadium — the smallest in baseball — and breaks from the trendy retro feel for a modern look with a steel and glass facade.

NACHO HELMET

with KEY LIMEADE

Being so close to the ocean, seafood is highly popular at Marlins Park. Add to that a thriving Central and South American populace, and you get specialties like ceviche, empanadas, and tamales. But for fans looking to fill their stomachs and take home a souvenir, the nacho helmet is the stadium's lead-off choice. Serve with Key limeade for a true taste of SoFlo.

NACHO HELMET

	PREP	COOK	MAKES
	5 MINUTES	**10** MINUTES	**4** HELMETS

	INGREDIENTS	
◇	1 pound	ground beef or turkey
◇	1 tablespoon	cumin
◇	1 tablespoon	chili powder
◇	1 teaspoon	paprika
◇	1 teaspoon	oregano
◇	1/4 teaspoon	cayenne pepper
◇	1 teaspoon	salt
◇	1/2 cup	water
◇	8 ounces	cheddar cheese
◇	1 15-ounce can	refried beans
◇	1 13-ounce bag	tortilla chips
◇	optional toppings: sour cream and	
◇	pico de gallo (see page 60)	

1 In a skillet over medium heat, brown the ground beef until no longer pink. Carefully drain fat.

2 Reduce heat to medium-low and add the cumin, chili powder, paprika, oregano, cayenne pepper, salt, and water. Bring to a simmer and cook for 10 minutes.

3 Meanwhile, grate the cheese and set aside.

4 Heat the refried beans in a saucepan over medium heat and set aside.

5 To assemble, spread the chips evenly in a helmet or on a platter. Pour the beans over the chips, followed by meat, cheese, and desired toppings.

6 Serve immediately.

HELMET HUNGER

The trend of serving food in batting helmets isn't new. In fact, ice cream sundae helmets were first served at ballparks in the early 1970s! The miniature plastic helmets quickly became fan collectables and an easy way for Major League teams to advertise their brands. Today, ice cream sundae helmets can be found at most MLB stadiums, but a few teams serve up megameals in full-sized batting helmets.

POUTINE HELMET
(Philadelphia Phillies, Citizens Bank Park)

Fries, cheese, bacon, and gravy served in plastic helmet.

KEY LIMEADE

PREP	COOK	MAKES
10 MINUTES	0 MINUTES	2 QUARTS

INGREDIENTS

◇	6 cups	water, divided
◇	1 ½ cups	granulated sugar
◇	2 cups	lime juice
◇	ice cubes and lime slices, for serving	
◇		

1 In a saucepan, combine 2 cups of water with the sugar and bring to a low boil over medium-high heat. Stir to dissolve the sugar, then remove from heat.

2 In a pitcher, combine the boiled sugar water, the other 4 cups of water, and lime juice. Stir well.

3 Serve in glasses with ice cubes and lime slices.

CHICHARRONES
(San Francisco Giants, AT&T Park)

Fried pork rinds served with chili-lime salt in a miniature plastic cap.

RIB BUCKET
(Chicago White Sox, U.S. Cellular Field)

Ribs, french fries, coleslaw, and cornbread served in a full-sized helmet.

NYM

New York Mets Baseball Club

CITI FIELD

LOCATION
Queens, New York
OPENED
2009
CAPACITY
41,922
NICKNAMES
New Shea

In the spring of 2009, the Mets moved from their original home, Shea Stadium, to the classically styled Citi Field. While a new ballpark, walking into Citi Field is like time traveling back to when the Dodgers and Giants dominated New York's playing fields. It's an old-fashioned, bowled-shaped park with red brick and limestone arches over the entrances. Nearly half of the seating is on the lower level, so fans can get an intimate view of the their favorite players. Of their two World Series, neither was won at Citi Field, but soon after the park opened, Mets outfielder Gary Sheffield blasted his 500th home run, and on June 1, 2012, pitcher Johan Santana threw the team's first ever no-hitter.

GARLIC FRIES

with CHOCOLATE-BANANA MILKSHAKE

Located in New York City's Queens borough, there are varied food options at Citi Field, from fried flounder to New York style pizza and Italian hero sandwiches. But one fave, garlic fries, is packed with nine innings worth of flavor. Pair them with a cool, creamy chocolate-banana milkshake for the perfect salty and sweet combination.

GARLIC FRIES

PREP	COOK	MAKES
10	**30**	**4**
MINUTES	MINUTES	SERVINGS

	INGREDIENTS	
◇	4	russet potatoes
◇	¼ cup	olive oil
◇	1 tablespoon	crushed garlic
◇	1 teaspoons	salt
◇	½ teaspoon	ground black pepper

1 Preheat oven to 450°F and line a baking sheet with parchment paper. Set aside.

2 Peel and cut the potatoes into ¼-inch wide sticks, like french fries. Dry well with a paper towel and place in mixing bowl with olive oil, crushed garlic, salt, and ground black pepper. Stir until the potatoes are coated.

3 Arrange the potatoes on the baking sheet and place in the oven for 15 minutes. Then flip them with a spatula and bake an additional 15 minutes or until golden brown and crispy.

4 Serve immediately.

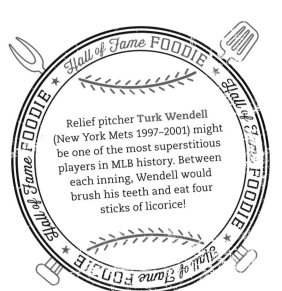

Hall of Fame FOODIE

Relief pitcher **Turk Wendell** (New York Mets 1997–2001) might be one of the most superstitious players in MLB history. Between each inning, Wendell would brush his teeth and eat four sticks of licorice!

CHOCOLATE-BANANA MILKSHAKE

PREP	COOK	MAKES
10	**0**	**2**
MINUTES	MINUTES	SHAKES

INGREDIENTS		
◇	2 cups	chocolate ice cream
◇	2	bananas, peeled
◇	½ cup	milk

1 Combine the ice cream, bananas, and milk in a blender. Blend until smooth.

2 Pour into glasses and serve cold.

New York City is known as the Big Apple, but Citi Field is home to one of the biggest apples in all of New York. The Home Run Apple (left), located in center field, stands sixteen-feet tall and weighs 4,800 pounds, significantly larger than the original apple from the old Shea Stadium (above) which is now on display outside Citi Field. When a Mets player hits a home run, the center-field apple lifts from its encasement and illuminates in celebration.

Philadelphia Phillies Baseball Club

CITIZENS BANK PARK

LOCATION	
Philadelphia, Pennsylvania	
OPENED	
2004	
CAPACITY	
43,651	
NICKNAMES	
The Bank	

Until the spring of 2004, the Phillies shared Veterans Stadium with the NFL's Eagles. But they joined many teams in the aughts that wanted wide-open, retro stadiums specifically for the baseball fan. Citizens Bank Park, the Phillies new home, is part of the South Philadelphia Sports Complex, which also includes the Eagles's new stadium, Lincoln Financial Field, and Wells Fargo Center, which hosts the NHL's Flyers and NBA's 76ers. Not only are the Phillies one of the MLB's oldest teams, having won two World Series (1980 and 2008), but the city itself is rich in history, housing the Liberty Bell at Independence Hall. Out in right-center field stands a 50-foot-tall replica of the Liberty Bell, and whenever a Philly slugs a home run, it swings and rings out.

PHILLY CHEESESTEAK SLIDERS

with CRABBY TOTS

The Philly cheesesteak is the signature sandwich of Philadelphia and the signature concession of Citizens Bank Park. With tender, juicy steak and melted mounds of cheese, there's a whole lot to love in this City of Brotherly Love classic. Pair them with these salty, seasoned tater tots, a fun twist on the stadium's famous Crabfries.

PHILLY CHEESESTEAK SLIDERS

PREP	COOK	MAKES
20 MINUTES	**10** MINUTES	**12** SLIDERS

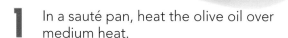

INGREDIENTS

◇	2 tablespoons	olive oil
◇	1 pound	London broil, sliced thinly
◇	½	onion, sliced thinly
◇	1	bell pepper, sliced thinly
◇	½ teaspoon	salt
◇	¼ teaspoon	black pepper
◇	½ cup	beef stock or broth
◇	12	slices provolone cheese
◇	12	slider buns

1. In a sauté pan, heat the olive oil over medium heat.

2. Add the sliced peppers and onions. Cook for about five minutes or until slightly softened.

3. Carefully add the meat without splattering. Stir well.

4. Add the beef stock or broth and turn the heat up to high.

5. Cook the meat for an additional 1–2 minutes or until most of the broth is evaporated. Set aside.

6. Open the slider buns and place them on a large sheet pan.

7. Using tongs, place an equal amount of meat, onion, and pepper on half of the buns.

8. Place a slice of cheese on top of the meat and place in the oven.

9. Turn on the broil function on the oven. Bake for about 3 minutes or until the cheese is melted and bubbly. Check often to avoid burning.

10. Place bun tops on the sandwiches and serve.

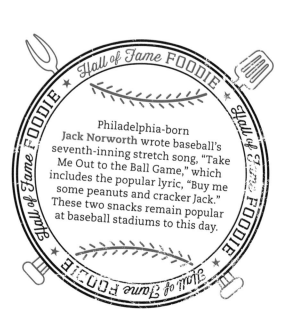

Hall of Fame FOODIE

Philadelphia-born **Jack Norworth** wrote baseball's seventh-inning stretch song, "Take Me Out to the Ball Game," which includes the popular lyric, "Buy me some peanuts and cracker Jack." These two snacks remain popular at baseball stadiums to this day.

CRABBY TOTS

PREP	COOK	MAKES
5 MINUTES	30 MINUTES	4 SERVINGS

	INGREDIENTS	
◇	1 pound	frozen tater tots
◇	1 tablespoon	olive oil
◇	2 tablespoons	Old Bay seasoning
◇		
◇		
◇		
◇		
◇		

1 Bake tater tots according to package directions on large baking sheet lined with parchment paper.

2 When the tots are done, place them into a large mixing bowl. Drizzle with olive oil and sprinkle with Old Bay seasoning and toss gently.

3 Serve immediately. Dip in cheesy dipping sauce (see page 99), if desired.

THE GREAT CHEESESTEAK DEBATE

Brothers Pat and Harry Olivieri, the founders of Pat's King of Steaks, served up the first Philly cheesesteak more than 85 years ago. There's no debating their history, but the city's favorite sandwich is the subject of heated arguments. In 1966, Joey Vento opened Geno's Steaks across the street. The two competing sandwich shops have been rivals ever since. Although their cheesesteaks are similar, one ingredient sets them apart: cheese! Pat's prefers Cheez Whiz while Geno's tops their sandwiches with provolone. Either way, food lovers can't lose.

 VS.

WAS

Washington Nationals Baseball Club

NATIONALS PARK

LOCATION
Washington, DC
OPENED
2008
CAPACITY
41,418

For more than 30 years, the nation's capital was without a baseball team. But that all changed in 2005, when the Montreal Expos relocated to Washington, DC, and switched names to the Nationals. A few years later, in 2008, Nationals Park opened. Unlike many new ball fields that try to capture those bygone days with a classic brick look, the Nationals's stadium has a sleek, modern feel with a glass and steel facade. From the stadium's upper deck, fans can glimpse the US Capitol Building.

CHILI CHEESE FRIES

with KETTLE CORN

Being the seat of the US government, DC attracts people from all over the world, so it's only fitting that Nationals Park offers a wide variety of food choices, from sushi to burritos, shawarmas, and more, representing the area's many ethnicities. But for fans who want that iconic Nationals Park treat, it's chili smothering hot dogs, spaghetti, nachos, or fries.

CHILI CHEESE FRIES

	PREP	COOK	MAKES
	10 MINUTES	**30** MINUTES	**4** SERVINGS

	INGREDIENTS	
◇	4	russet potatoes
◇	¼ cup	olive oil
◇	1 teaspoon	salt
◇	½ teaspoon	ground black pepper
◇	4 ounces	cheddar cheese
◇	1 recipe	chili from Coney Dogs
◇		(see page 42)

1 Preheat oven to 450°F and line a baking sheet with parchment paper. Set aside.

2 Peel and cut the potatoes into ¼-inch wide sticks, like french fries. Dry well with a paper towel and place in mixing bowl with olive oil, salt, and ground black pepper. Stir until the potatoes are coated.

3 Arrange the potatoes on the baking sheet and place in the oven for 15 minutes, then flip them with a spatula and bake an additional 15 minutes or until golden brown and crispy.

4 To assemble, place fries on a plate, followed by chili, and sprinkle with cheese.

5 Serve immediately.

EVERY DAY IS FRY DAY!

There are enough french fry varieties throughout the Major Leagues for a whole week of fry days.

MONDAY

Chili Cheese Fries at Nationals Park
(Washington Nationals)

TUESDAY

Garlic Fries at Citi Field
(New York Mets)

WEDNESDAY

Poutine Fries at Rogers Centre
(Toronto Blue Jays)

KETTLE CORN

	PREP	COOK	MAKES
	5 MINUTES	**5** MINUTES	**4** SERVINGS

	INGREDIENTS	
◇	¼ cup	oil
◇	¼ cup	granulated sugar
◇	½ cup	popping corn

1 In a saucepan over medium-high heat, add the oil and sugar. When the oil is hot, add the popping corn and place the lid on top of the saucepan.

2 When the corn begins popping, start sliding the pan over the burner back and forth to keep the sugar from burning.

3 Pop the corn for about 2 minutes or until the popping slows down. Continue sliding the pan for another minute or two before transferring to a serving bowl.

4 Serve immediately. Store leftovers in an airtight container at room temperature for up to 1 day.

Hall of Fame FOODIE

In 2011, relief pitcher **Drew Storen** (Washington Nationals 2010–present) ate a grilled cheese sandwich with a glass of milk every day throughout the season.

THURSDAY
Disco Fries
at Yankee Stadium
(New York Yankees)

FRIDAY
Carne Asada Fries
at Petco Park
(San Diego Padres)

SATURDAY
Crabfries
at Citizens Bank Park
(Philadelphia Phillies)

SUNDAY
Plain French Fries, available everywhere!

CHC

Chicago Cubs Baseball Club

WRIGLEY FIELD

LOCATION
Chicago, Illinois
OPENED
1914
CAPACITY
41,160
NICKNAMES
The Friendly Confines
Cubs Park

When it comes to pure history and atmosphere, few ballparks can compete with the "friendly confines" of Wrigley Field. Built in 1914, this gem on the north side of Chicago has been home to more than a century of professional baseball. Wrigley's outfield fence — brick covered with thick green ivy — is its hallmark. By modern standards, the stadium is small, seating just more than 40,000. But some of the most prized seating isn't even in the stadium, as adjacent buildings offer fans "rooftop seating" that allows them to look in on ball games without ever entering the park!

PRETZEL TWISTS

with HONEY MUSTARD & CHEESY DIPPING SAUCES

Whether inside the stadium or in the streets of surrounding Wrigleyville, fans have a wide range of food choices. From juicy Chicago-style hot dogs and deep-dish pizza to Wrigley's famous giant twist pretzel, complete with cheesy dipping sauce. The food on the north side of Chicago is hearty and delicious.

PRETZEL TWISTS

PREP	COOK	MAKES
1¼ MINUTES	30 MINUTES	6 TWISTS

	INGREDIENTS	
◇	1 packet	instant yeast
◇	2 tablespoons	salt
◇	1 teaspoon	honey
◇	1 cup	warm water
◇	2 ½ cups	flour, plus more for kneading
◇	3 cups	water
◇	½ cup	baking soda
◇		vegetable oil spray
◇	6 tablespoons	melted butter
◇	optional sprinklings: kosher salt, poppy seeds,	
◇	sesame seeds	

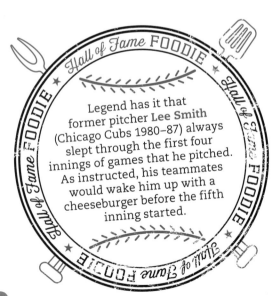

Legend has it that former pitcher **Lee Smith** (Chicago Cubs 1980–87) always slept through the first four innings of games that he pitched. As instructed, his teammates would wake him up with a cheeseburger before the fifth inning started.

1 In a large mixing bowl, combine the yeast, salt, honey, and warm water. Allow to sit 2 minutes.

2 Add the flour. Mix well and turn the bowl onto a floured surface. Knead the dough well with your hands for about 5 minutes, or until it is soft and smooth.

3 Spray the inside of a clean mixing bowl with vegetable oil spray and place the dough in the bowl. Cover with a clean damp cloth and allow to sit for 30 minutes to rise.

4 Flour a surface and place the dough on it. Knead 1 minute, then cut the dough into 6 pieces.

5 Roll the dough between your hands and the counter to make ropes about 12 inches long.

6 Fold a rope in half and then twist it to make the dough braided. Repeat for remaining dough and set aside.

7 Preheat your oven to 400°F. Spray the baking sheet with a light coating of vegetable oil spray.

8 Boil water in a saucepan. Add baking soda and stir until it dissolves. Reduce the heat so it slowly simmers. Drop the twists in the saucepan two at a time. Let them cook for 30 seconds.

9 Place the twists ¼-inch apart on the baking sheet. Sprinkle with salt and seeds, if desired.

10 Bake for 15 minutes or until golden brown. Then brush with melted butter before serving.

HONEY-MUSTARD DIPPING SAUCE

PREP	COOK	MAKES
5	**0**	**1½**
MINUTES	MINUTES	CUPS

INGREDIENTS	
◇	1 cup	coarse ground mustard
◇	1/2 cup	honey
◇	1 teaspoon	salt
◇		

1 Combine all of the ingredients in a mixing bowl.

2 Taste the mixture and add more honey or mustard if needed. Serve alongside your pretzel twists.

CHEESY DIPPING SAUCE

PREP	COOK	MAKES
5	**5**	**1**
MINUTES	MINUTES	CUP

INGREDIENTS	
◇	2 ounces	sharp cheddar cheese
◇	1 tablespoon	butter
◇	1 tablespoon	all-purpose flour
◇	1 cup	milk
◇	½ teaspoon	salt
◇	½ teaspoon	paprika
◇		

1 Grate the cheese and set aside. In a saucepan over medium heat, melt the butter and add the flour. Whisk gently until the flour absorbs the butter.

2 Slowly pour in the milk while whisking quickly.

3 As the liquid thickens, add the cheese, salt, and paprika, stirring frequently until the cheese completely melts.

4 Pour into a serving bowl and serve immediately.

CIN

GREAT AMERICAN BALL PARK

LOCATION
Cincinnati, Ohio
OPENED
2003
CAPACITY
42,319
NICKNAMES
GABP

With a name like the Great American Ball Park, you'd expect a lot out of the Cincinnati Reds's home. And it doesn't disappoint. At 40 feet tall and 138 feet wide, the GABP can brag about having one of the largest HD scoreboards in baseball and is that classic, bowl-shaped ballpark that today's fans love in their home fields. The Reds began playing ball at GABP in 2003, with Reds superstar Ken Griffey Jr. getting the first hit, a double. The Reds are one of the oldest teams, joining the National League way back in 1882. And fans take pride in their team's history, which includes five World Series wins. The Reds Hall of Fame Museum sits next door to the park and at GABP's main entrance is Crosely Terrace, where fans are greeted by statues of great players from bygone days, including Frank Robinson, Ted Kluszewski, and Johnny Bench.

CINCINNATI-STYLE CHILI

with COLOSSAL COOKIE SUNDAE

If you're hungry, there are few better parks to fill up in, starting with topped fries. They can come covered in smoked chicken, pulled pork, or cheese and hot sauce. Cincinnati is also renowned for its chili, and it's used to cover everything from fries to spaghetti

CINCINNATI-STYLE CHILI

PREP	COOK	MAKES
15	**30**	**4**
MINUTES	MINUTES	SERVINGS

INGREDIENTS

◇	1	small onion
◇	1 tablespoon	olive oil
◇	1 pound	ground beef or turkey
◇	1 15-ounce can	tomato sauce
◇	1 ½ cups	beef broth
◇	4 tablespoons	chili powder
◇	1 teaspoon	cumin
◇	¼ teaspoon	allspice
◇	¼ teaspoon	ground cloves
◇	½ teaspoon	ground cinnamon
◇	1 teaspoon	unsweetened cocoa powder
◇	½ teaspoon	paprika
◇	1 tablespoon + 1 teaspoon	salt, divided
◇	8 ounces	spaghetti noodles
◇	8 ounces	cheddar cheese
◇		
◇		
◇		
◇		
◇		
◇		
◇		

1 Chop the onion into small pieces and set aside.

2 In a medium-sized pot, heat the olive oil over medium heat. Add the onions and stir occasionally for about 5 minutes or until they begin to soften.

3 Add the meat, breaking it up with a spoon as it cooks.

4 When the meat has browned, add the tomato sauce, beef broth, chili powder, cumin, allspice, ground cloves, ground cinnamon, cocoa powder, paprika, and 1 teaspoon salt. Stir to combine and bring to a simmer.

5 Reduce heat to medium-low and simmer for 20 minutes, stirring occasionally.

6 Meanwhile, fill a large pot with water and add 1 tablespoon salt. Place on a burner over high heat until it begins to boil. Add the pasta and cook until just tender, about 8 minutes. Drain through a colander. Set aside.

7 Grate the cheese and set aside. To assemble, place some pasta on a plate, followed by 1 cup of the chili, and sprinkle with ¼ cup cheese. Serve immediately.

COLOSSAL COOKIE SUNDAE

	PREP	COOK	MAKES
	5 MINUTES	**0** MINUTES	**1** SUNDAE

	INGREDIENTS	
◇	3 scoops	cookie dough ice cream
◇	3	chocolate-vanilla crème
◇		sandwich cookies
◇	¼ cup	chocolate syrup
◇	¼ cup	caramel sauce
◇	1	maraschino cherry

1 Place the scoops of ice cream in a bowl.

2 Crumble the cookies in your hands and sprinkle over the ice cream.

3 Drizzle the sauces over the top, followed by cherry. Serve immediately.

CHILI CAPITAL OF THE WORLD

Cincinnati is sometimes referred to as the "Chili Capital of the World." More than 250 chili restaurants operate throughout the city, and residents consume more than two million pounds of chili annually! In the early 20th century, Macedonian and Greek immigrants arrived in New York. Some entrepreneurs opened hot dog stands, topping their specialty dogs with Turkish-spiced chili. The chili dogs, later known as Coney Dogs, made their way to the Midwest, from Cincinnati to Detroit. Eventually, the chili itself made its way atop a pile of spaghetti, the origins of which are often disputed. Unlike Texas-style chili, beans are not included, while sweet and spicy flavors of cloves, cinnamon, and cocoa dominate the chili's unique flavor.

MIL

Milwaukee Brewers Baseball Club

MILLER PARK

LOCATION
Milwaukee, Wisconsin
OPENED
2001
CAPACITY
41,900

In the spring of 2001, the Brewers joined the handful of teams playing in a stadium with a retractable roof. And like the team itself, Miller Stadium is named after one of Milwaukee's most famous industries: Miller Brewing Company. The stadium showcases a huge scoreboard in center field, and over in left field is Bernie's Dugout, home of the Brewer's mascot. Every time a Brewer slams a home run, Bernie celebrates by sliding down from his perch. Walking through the home plate entrance, fans are greeted by statues of some of the greats to don a Brewer uniform, like Robin Yount and Hank Aaron, as well as longtime radio announcer Bob Uecker.

BRATWURST SLIDERS

with CHEESE PUFFS

Along with the brewing industry, Wisconsin is known for cheese and bratwurst. And both come in abundance at Miller Stadium, from fried cheese curds to the 18-inch Down Wisconsin Avenue Brat. To take their love of sausages even further, the sixth inning features a Sausage Race, in which five people in sausage costumes run around the park.

BRATWURST SLIDERS

PREP	COOK	MAKES
30 MINUTES	**10** MINUTES	**12** SLIDERS

	INGREDIENTS	
◇	6	fresh bratwursts
◇	1	onion
◇	1 tablespoon	olive oil
◇	1 teaspoon	salt
◇	½ teaspoon	black pepper
◇	12	pretzel slider buns
◇	optional toppings: honey-mustard dipping sauce	
◇	(see page 99) and/or sauerkraut	

1 Carefully score the casing of the bratwurst lengthwise. Peel the casing off and discard.

2 Cut each sausage link in half. Use your hands to form the meat into patties.

3 Slice the onion thinly and set aside. Heat olive oil in a large skillet over medium heat and add the sliced onions. Stir, then sprinkle a little salt and pepper in the pan. Cook until the onions are softened and slightly golden brown. Remove from pan and set aside.

4 Using the same pan, turn the heat to medium and add the bratwurst patties, working in batches if necessary. Cook for about 3–4 minutes per side, or until each side is browned and cooked in the middle.

5 Open the pretzel bun and place a bratwurst burger on the bottom. Add about 2 tablespoons of onion. You can also add sauerkraut on top of the onions.

6 Spread 1 tablespoon of the honey mustard on the inside of the top half of the pretzel bun. Place the top half of the bun on top and serve on a platter.

TOP SAUSAGE

Miller Park is the only Major League ballpark where sausages — including brats and Polish and Italian sausages — outsell hot dogs! Sausage sales are nearly double the sales of hot dogs annually.

CHEESE PUFFS

PREP	COOK	MAKES
5 MINUTES	**20** MINUTES	**1** QUART

INGREDIENTS

◇	1 17.3-ounce package	frozen puff pastry, thawed
◇		
◇	32	cheese curds
◇	1	egg
◇	2 tablespoons	cool water

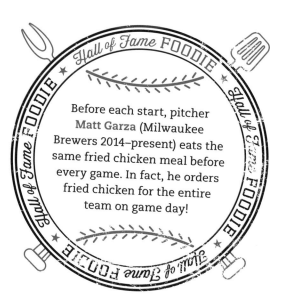

Hall of Fame FOODIE

Before each start, pitcher **Matt Garza** (Milwaukee Brewers 2014–present) eats the same fried chicken meal before every game. In fact, he orders fried chicken for the entire team on game day!

1 Preheat oven to 400°F and line a baking sheet with parchment paper. Set aside.

2 Begin cutting the first pastry sheet by slicing it into 16 equal squares. Repeat for the second sheet.

3 Place a cheese curd in the lower right corner of each square.

4 Whisk the egg in a mixing bowl with the water.

5 Brush the egg wash onto the edges of the squares on all sides.

6 Starting from the right corner, start rolling dough over the cheese curd, folding in the sides as you roll. Press the edges to seal and set on the baking sheet. Repeat for the rest of the squares.

7 Brush the remaining egg wash on top of the dough and place in the oven for 20 minutes, check on them after 15 minutes.

8 When they are golden brown, remove from the oven and allow to cool for about 5 minutes before serving.

PIT

Pittsburgh Pirates Baseball Club

PNC PARK

LOCATION	
Pittsburgh, Pennsylvania	
OPENED	
2001	
CAPACITY	
38,362	
NICKNAMES	
The Park	

For 30 years, the Pirates shared a stadium with the NFL's Steelers. But like many other teams in the aughts, they moved to a park dedicated solely to baseball. PNC Park opened in the spring of 2001. The Pirates are one of the oldest teams in baseball, joining the National League in 1882. In their more than 100-year history, they've won five World Series. But the new park hasn't brought them any luck yet. While a Pittsburgh native, Sean Casey, got the park's first hit, a home run over right-center, he was playing for the Reds at the time. PNC Park is one of the smallest ballparks, seating just fewer than 40,000 fans. Still, it is worth visiting for the amazing views of the Pittsburgh skyline and the Roberto Clemente Bridge, named after one of the team's greats.

SPICY PITTSBURGH-STYLE SANDWICH

with PEANUT BUTTER CUP FUDGE

Pittsburgh is known for its hard-working, blue-collar folks, and what better reward for a long day on the job than a hearty sandwich? The city's favorite sandwich shop, Primanti Brothers, has dozens of restaurants across Pennsylvania, including inside PNC Park. This Pittsburgh-style sandwich is stuffed with meat, coleslaw, and french fries.

SPICY PITTSBURGH-STYLE SANDWICH

PREP	COOK	MAKES
5	**30**	**4**
MINUTES	MINUTES	SANDWICHES

INGREDIENTS

◇	2 cups	frozen french fries
◇	1	French bread loaf
◇	1 pound	sliced hot capicola ham
◇	8	slices provolone cheese
◇	8	leaves lettuce
◇	4 tablespoons	mayonnaise, divided

1 Place french fries on a parchment-paper-lined baking sheet and bake according to package directions.

2 Meanwhile, cut the French bread into 4 equal pieces, then slice horizontally.

3 Place the meat in a large skillet over medium-high heat. Turn the meat frequently to prevent sticking.

4 When the meat is slightly browned, divide it equally among the bottom halves of the four sandwiches.

5 Top with provolone cheese, ½ cup of french fries, and 2 lettuce leaves.

6 Spread 1 tablespoon of mayonnaise on each of the top halves and place on top of the sandwiches. Serve immediately.

KETCHUP KING

Baseball and hot dogs go hand in hand, and some believe hot dogs and ketchup do too! Ketchup devotees owe a lot to Pittsburgh. The city is home to Heinz, maker of America's bestselling ketchup. In fact, Heinz Stadium is home to Pittsburgh's other beloved sports team, the Steelers.

PEANUT BUTTER CUP FUDGE

PREP	COOK	MAKES
10	**4**	**16**
MINUTES	HOURS	PIECES

INGREDIENTS

◇	2 tablespoons	unsalted butter, divided
◇	1 14-ounce can	sweetened condensed
◇		milk, divided
◇	2 cups	semisweet chocolate chips
◇	1 cup	peanut butter chips
◇	generous sprays	cooking spray

All-Star pitcher **Tim Wakefield** (Pittsburgh Pirates 1992–1993) reportedly ate a pound of spaghetti before games he started.

1 Generously spray a baking dish with cooking spray and set aside.

2 In a microwave-safe bowl, combine 1 ½ tablespoons butter, 1 ¼ cups sweetened condensed milk, and the semisweet chocolate chips. Microwave at 50% power for 30 seconds. Stir with a spatula and microwave for an additional 30 seconds or until the chocolate is melted and smooth.

3 Pour the mixture in the baking dish and spread evenly.

4 Working quickly, combine ½ tablespoon butter, ½ cup sweetened condensed milk, and the peanut butter chips in a second microwave-safe bowl. Microwave at 50% power for 30 seconds. Stir with a spatula and microwave for an additional 30 seconds or until chips are melted and smooth.

5 Pour the mixture over the top of the chocolate and spread evenly. Place in refrigerator for at least 4 hours.

6 To serve, cut into 16 squares. Serve cooled or at room temperature. Store leftovers in an airtight container in refrigerator for up to 1 week.

STL

St. Louis Cardinals Baseball Club

BUSCH STADIUM

LOCATION
St. Louis, Missouri
OPENED
2006
CAPACITY
43,975
NICKNAMES
Busch Stadium III

The Cardinals must really like the name of their stadium because every park in which they have played has been called "Busch Stadium." They were all named after Gussie Busch who bought the team in 1953. The latest incarnation of Busch Stadium opened in April 2006, so it is one of the newest stadiums in baseball. But its grass field and openness give it a classic baseball feel. Which is only fitting, as over the outfield wall, fans get a view of the Gateway Arch, a landmark as iconically American as baseball. The Cardinals quickly put their stadium to good use, winning a World Series the same year it opened, and then one more in 2011.

TOASTED RAVIOLI

with MARINARA SAUCE

Every ballpark has its signature food — the one thing every fan and visitor must try to make their visit complete. At Busch Stadium, that's toasted ravioli and toasted cannelloni. These crispy treats are stuffed with meat and cheese, and then fans dip them in steamy

TOASTED RAVIOLI

	PREP	COOK	MAKES
	10 MINUTES	5 MINUTES	4 SERVINGS

	INGREDIENTS	
◇	1 cup	all-purpose flour
◇	2	eggs
◇	1 cup	Italian-seasoned
◇		bread crumbs
◇	16	refrigerated raviolis
◇	½ cup	olive oil
◇	1 recipe	marinara sauce
◇		

1 Create your breading station: place flour on 1 plate, eggs on a second plate, and bread crumbs on a third. Whisk the eggs with a fork.

2 Roll a ravioli in the flour, then dip in egg, letting the excess drip off. Finally, roll the ravioli in the bread crumbs. Set on a plate or cutting board. Repeat for the rest of the raviolis.

3 In a skillet, heat the olive oil over medium heat.

4 When the oil is hot, carefully place about 4 raviolis in the skillet.

5 Cook for about 2 minutes or until golden brown. Carefully turn the raviolis over to cook the other side for an additional 2 minutes.

6 Transfer to a paper-towel-lined plate to drain.

7 Repeat in batches.

8 Serve hot with marinara sauce for dipping.

STADIUM FARE

Busch Stadium is one of five Major League Baseball ballparks to be named after food or drink companies:

1. BUSCH STADIUM
2. COORS FIELD
3. MILLER PARK
4. MINUTE MAID PARK
5. TROPICANA FIELD

MARINARA SAUCE

PREP	COOK	MAKES
5 MINUTES	10 MINUTES	1 SERVING

	INGREDIENTS	
◇	1 teaspoon	olive oil
◇	1 teaspoon	crushed garlic
◇	1/4 teaspoon	crushed red pepper
◇		flakes
◇	8 ounces	crushed tomatoes
◇	1 teaspoon	salt
◇	1 teaspoon	sugar
◇	1 teaspoon	dried basil

1 In a skillet, heat the olive oil over medium heat.

2 Add garlic and red pepper flakes. Stir and cook for 1 minute.

3 Pour the crushed tomatoes in the skillet, along with the salt, sugar, and basil.

4 Bring to a simmer and cook for 10 minutes.

LEGENDARY *Pasta*

St. Louis's Most Valuable Pasta has Hall of Fame origins! Toasted ravioli originated in a part of the city called The Hill, sometime called "America's Other Little Italy." Two Major League catchers, future Hall-of-Famer Yogi Berra and Joe Garagiola (St. Louis Cardinals 1946–1951), grew up on The Hill as neighbors and young competitors, both entering professional baseball in 1946. In fact, one legend says that Garagiola's older brother, Mickey Garagiola, was working as a waiter on the day toasted ravioli was first made. On that day, a chef accidently dropped ravioli into boiling oil instead of boiling water. Instead of throwing them away, the chef served them up, and a St. Louis favorite was born!

Arizona Diamondbacks Baseball Club

CHASE FIELD

LOCATION
Phoenix, Arizona
OPENED
1998
CAPACITY
48,519
NICKNAMES
The BOB
The Snake Pit
The Aircraft Hangar

The Diamondbacks are one of the youngest teams in the MLB, joining the National League in 1998. So of course they had to have one of the best and largest scoreboards, standing 47 feet tall, and one of the coolest stadiums in the league. And they literally needed it. On those sunny summer days, Arizona's sweltering heat would be unbearable for players and fans alike. Chase Field was the first baseball park to have both a retractable roof, which is closed during those hot day games and open for the cooler night games, and a grass field. The cool, new stadium must have been lucky for the Diamondbacks. Shortly after entering the MLB, they won a World Series (2001). And no wonder, they had the Big Unit, Randy Johnson, on the mound that year.

ARIZONA HOT DOG

with SOPAIPILLAS

A trendy new stadium deserves some trendy new eats. So think food trucks. Food Truck Alley features different food trucks every game, with many eats having a southwestern flare. For fans with a sweet tooth, there is the churro dog, topped with frozen yogurt,

ARIZONA HOT DOG

PREP	COOK	MAKES
15 MINUTES	5 MINUTES	4 DOGS

	INGREDIENTS	
◇	4	slices bacon
◇	1	small tomato
◇	1	small onion
◇	4 ounces	cheddar cheese
◇	4	hot dog buns
◇	4 tablespoons	salsa verde, divided
◇	4 teaspoons	mayonnaise, divided
◇	1 teaspoon	hot sauce, divided

1 In a skillet over medium heat, fry the bacon until crisp. Remove and set aside.

2 In a second skillet, add hot dogs and 3 cups water. Simmer over medium heat for 5 minutes or until hot.

3 While the hot dogs are cooking, chop the onion and tomato into small pieces and set aside.

4 Grate the cheese and set aside.

5 To assemble the hot dogs, place hot dogs in the buns, followed by a slice of bacon on each. Sprinkle 1 tablespoon of tomato, followed by 1 tablespoon onion, 1 tablespoon salsa verde, and drizzle 1 teaspoon mayonnaise, and a ¼ teaspoon hot sauce on each hot dog. Top with cheese before serving.

The popularity of mobile food trucks has exploded across the country, and the Arizona Diamondbacks are capitalizing on this trend — to the benefit of hungry fans! On weekends, a rotating schedule of Phoenix's all-star food trucks park just outside Gate A at Chase Field. With local options from grilled cheese sandwiches to quesadillas to signature burgers, Diamondback fans never have to eat the same thing twice!

SOPAIPILLAS

PREP	COOK	MAKES
5 MINUTES	**5** MINUTES	**4** PIECES

	INGREDIENTS	
◇	4	small flour tortillas
◇	½ cup	granulated sugar
◇	2 teaspoons	ground cinnamon
◇	4 tablespoons	oil

1 Cut the tortillas into wedges. Set aside.

2 In a mixing bowl, combine the sugar and cinnamon. Stir well and set aside.

3 In a skillet, heat the oil over medium-high heat.

4 Working in batches, add some tortillas. Cook for about 30 seconds and turn over carefully with a tongs. Cook an additional 30 seconds.

5 Carefully remove from the hot oil to a space lined with paper towels to drain.

6 Allow to cool slightly before dipping in the cinnamon sugar.

7 Serve warm. Store leftovers in an airtight container at room temperature for up to 1 day.

What's the Count?

The United States Department of Agriculture recommends a daily intake of 2,640 calories for men and 1,785 calories for women. So what's the calorie count on some baseball classics?

	Calories
Foot-long Hot Dog	475
Cotton Candy	225
Corn Dog	450
Peanuts (1 ounce)	125
Soft Pretzel	390

COL

Colorado Rockies Baseball Club

COORS FIELD

LOCATION
Denver, Colorado
OPENED
1995
CAPACITY
50,398
NICKNAMES
Jurassic Park

In 1991, the Colorado Rockies were selected to be one of two expansion teams to join the MLB. The team initially shared Mile High Stadium with the NFL's Broncos until Coors Field opened in the spring of 1995. With the thin mountain air, the park is known as a hitters park, in which sluggers like Todd Helton, Larry Walker, and Carlos Gonzalez have thrived. The Rockies' stadium is built in downtown Denver, but to keep it from towering over nearby buildings, Coors Field is set 21 feet below street level. A purple row of seats wrapping around the stadium — twenty rows up on the upper deck — marks one mile above sea level.

ROCKY MOUNTAIN BURRITO

with CHOCOLATY BERRY KABOBS

Coors Field is said to have one of the best burgers in baseball, the Helton burger, named after one of the team's most-beloved players. Hot dogs are taken to a new level at Xtreme Dog, whose dogs are topped with everything from bacon to chili sauce. But those looking to stuff themselves look no further than this overstuffed Rocky Mountain Burrito!

ROCKY MOUNTAIN BURRITOS

PREP	COOK	MAKES
5 MINUTES	**30** MINUTES	**4** BURRITOS

	INGREDIENTS	
◇	generous sprays	cooking spray
◇	1	medium onion
◇	1 tablespoon	olive oil
◇	1 pound	lean ground beef or
◇		turkey
◇	2 teaspoons	crushed garlic
◇	1 teaspoon	salt
◇	1 teaspoon	cumin
◇	2 teaspoons	chili powder
◇	1 teaspoon	smoked paprika
◇	1 8-ounce can	diced green chiles,
◇		drained
◇	1 8-ounce can	Mexican tomato sauce
◇	1 15-ounce can	pinto beans in chili sauce
◇	8 ounces	Monterey Jack cheese
◇	4 burrito-sized	flour tortillas
◇	optional toppings: guacamole (see page 65),	
◇	sour cream, and salsa	
◇		
◇		

1 Preheat oven to 425°F. Spray baking dish with cooking spray and set aside.

2 Chop the onion into small pieces and place in a skillet with olive oil over medium heat. Cook for about 5 minutes, stirring occasionally.

3 Add meat, breaking up gently with a spoon as it cooks.

4 When the meat is browned, add the crushed garlic, salt, cumin, chili powder, smoked paprika, diced green chiles, Mexican tomato sauce, and pinto beans.

5 Bring to a simmer and reduce heat to medium-low. Simmer for about 15 minutes.

6 While the filling simmers, grate the cheese and set aside.

7 When the filling is simmered, scoop out about 1 cup of the filling into each of the tortillas, then roll up, folding in the sides as well. Place them seam-side down in the baking dish.

8 Pour the remaining filling over the top of the burritos, then sprinkle with the cheese.

9 Place in the oven for about 10 minutes or until slightly browned.

10 Serve hot with fixings such as guacamole, sour cream, or salsa.

CHOCOLATY BERRY KABOBS

PREP	COOK	MAKES
10 MINUTES	0 MINUTES	8 KABOBS

INGREDIENTS	
6	large strawberries
24	blueberries
24	raspberries
2 ounces	chocolate almond bark

1 Place a large sheet of parchment paper on a flat surface.

2 Cut the tops off of each strawberry, then cut in quarters. Set aside.

3 Thread each skewer with 1 blueberry, followed by a raspberry, then a strawberry. Repeat 2 more times on each skewer.

4 Place finished skewers on parchment paper and set aside.

5 In a microwave-safe dish, heat the chocolate almond bark in the microwave at 50% power in 30 second increments until melted, stirring in between.

6 When the chocolate is melted, dip a fork in the chocolate and drizzle all over the kabobs.

7 Allow chocolate to cool before serving.

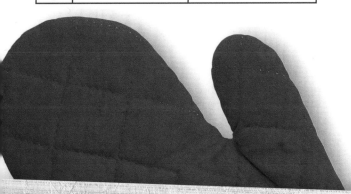

MILE-HIGH MEALS

Playing baseball at 5,280 feet is not without its difficulties. In 2002, the Colorado Rockies installed a humidor at Coors Field. The team stores baseballs inside the humidor to combat Denver's low humidity, which can make baseballs travel farther. Keeping baseballs at a constant 70 degrees and 50 percent humidity has helped reduce the relatively high number of home runs at the stadium.

When cooking at high elevations, chefs have to switch up their game plan too! At a mile above sea level, water boils at a lower temperature, so steamed or boiled foods take longer to cook. Baked goods often rise quickly, then fall. To combat this, increase baking temperatures by 15–25 degrees Fahrenheit.

LAD

Los Angeles Dodgers Baseball Club

DODGER STADIUM

LOCATION
Los Angeles, California
OPENED
1962
CAPACITY
56,000
NICKNAMES
Chavez Ravine
Blue Heaven On Earth

Along with the Giants, the Dodgers left New York in 1958 to find a new home in sunny California. Soon after, the city of Los Angeles had a new stadium built for their new baseball team. Opening April 10, 1962, Dodger Stadium is the third oldest MLB park currently in use. That means a lot of baseball history has happened here, including four of the Dodgers' six World Series titles. And some of the sport's greatest players have called Dodger Stadium home at one point during their careers, including pitchers Sandy Koufax and Don Sutton, and catcher Mike Piazza.

SOCAL HOT DOG

with MEXICAN CORN ON THE COB & BERRY-GRAPE COOLER

Like the local culture, the area's food is influenced by a large Hispanic population. Elote, Mexican corn on the cob with cheese and chili, is a must try to complete any Dodger Stadium experience. Carne asada nachos served in a plastic helmet is another fan fave. However, the simple yet uniquely sized, 10-inch hot dog is Dodger Stadium's bestseller.

SOCAL HOT DOG

PREP	COOK	MAKES
5	**5**	**4**
MINUTES	MINUTES	DOGS

	INGREDIENTS	
◇	4	hot dogs
◇	4 tablespoons	sweet pickle relish,
◇		divided
◇	4 teaspoons	yellow mustard
◇	4	hot dog buns

1 In a skillet, add the hot dogs with 3 cups water. Heat to simmering over medium heat. Cook for 5 minutes or until hot.

2 To assemble hot dog, place a hot dog in a bun, followed by 1 tablespoon of sweet pickle relish. Drizzle 1 teaspoon yellow mustard on top. Repeat for remaining hot dogs.

CITY OF HOT DOGS

In 2015, the National Hot Dog and Sausage Council predicted that Dodger Stadium would sell more hot dogs than any other Major League park. The more than 2.5 million hot dogs puts Dodger fans one million dogs above the next closest ballpark, Yankee Stadium. Most hot dogs sold at Dodger Stadium are "Dodger Dogs," a beloved 10-inch frankfurter that remains as simple and classic as when it was introduced in 1962.

MEXICAN CORN ON THE COB

PREP	COOK	MAKES
5 MINUTES	10 MINUTES	8 PIECES

	INGREDIENTS	
◇	8 ears	frozen sweet corn
◇	4 ounces	Mexican cheese, such
◇		as cotija
◇	8 tablespoons	mayonnaise, divided
◇	optional sprinklings: salt, pepper, and paprika	
◇		
◇		

1 Fill a large pot with water and bring to a boil. Add corn and reduce heat to simmering. Cook until tender, about 8 minutes.

2 Meanwhile, grate the cheese and set aside.

3 When the corn is cooked, remove carefully with a tongs. Allow to cool slightly before finishing, about 2 minutes.

4 Carefully spread 1 tablespoon of mayonnaise on each ear of corn. Sprinkle cheese generously all over the corn, followed by a dash of salt, pepper, and paprika. Serve hot.

BERRY-GRAPE COOLER

PREP	COOK	MAKES
5 MINUTES	0 MINUTES	2 QUARTS

	INGREDIENTS	
◇	2 cups	mixed berry juice
◇	2 cups	grape juice
◇	1 quart	lemon-lime soda
◇		ice cubes

1 In a pitcher, combine the mixed berry juice, grape juice, and lemon-lime soda. Stir well.

2 Serve in glasses with ice cubes.

PETCO PARK

LOCATION
San Diego, California
OPENED
2004
CAPACITY
41,164

The Padres shared a stadium with the NFL's Chargers until the opening of the 2004 season. That spring, they began playing in Petco Park, and celebrated their new-home opener with a win over in-state rivals, the Giants. Initially considered a great pitchers park — Trevor Hoffman threw a record-setting 500th career save here on June 6, 2007 — the outfield walls have since been moved in to help batters. The stadium captures the near-tropic feel of Southern California. The area around the park is landscaped with jacaranda and palm trees, and the main walkway up to the park has a stairway waterfall. Just outside the park's center-field wall is "Park at the Park," a grassy area where families can sit on blankets and view a game as if they were hanging out in their own backyards.

FISH TACOS

with CHIPOTLE MAYO & SPARKLING MINT LEMONADE

While the park offers the typical baseball fare, like hot dogs and peanuts, its food choices are heavily influenced by the area's Latino culture. Carne asada, fish tacos, and burritos are popular treats at the park.

FISH TACOS

PREP	COOK	MAKES
10	**10**	**6**
MINUTES	MINUTES	TACOS

	INGREDIENTS	
◇	1 pound	firm white fish,
◇		such as cod
◇	1 tablespoon	lime juice
◇	1 tablespoon	olive oil
◇	1 tablespoon	cumin
◇	1 teaspoon	salt
◇	1/4 teaspoon	cayenne pepper
◇	6	flour tortillas
◇	optional toppings: chipotle mayo, sour cream,	
◇	grated cheese, and lettuce	

1 Cut the fish into 2-inch cubes and place in a shallow baking dish.

2 In a small mixing bowl, combine the lime juice, olive oil, cumin, salt, and pepper. Whisk well and pour over the fish. Allow to marinate for 5 minutes.

3 In a skillet over medium heat, add the fish and marinade. Using tongs, carefully turn the pieces over after 3 minutes. Then cook another 3–4 minutes or until cooked through.

4 Evenly place fish on 6 tortillas, followed by chipotle mayo and desired garnishes. Serve immediately.

SOCAL KEEPS IT
LOCAL

In 2015, the Natural Resources Defense Council and the Green Sports Alliance recognized the San Diego Padres as "Champions of Game Day Food." The accolades are well deserved. More than 95 percent of the concession stands and restaurants within Petco Park get their food from Southern California. Locally sourced foods greatly reduce transportation costs and waste but also increase food freshness within the park. Even baseball's greatest classics, like hot dogs, hamburgers, and nachos, come from local sources. The Padres also donate uneaten food to nearby shelters, create biofuels from cooking oils, and find other innovative practices to keep baseball — and its food — sustainable for years to come.

CHIPOTLE MAYO

PREP	COOK	MAKES
5	0	1
MINUTES	HOUR	CUP

INGREDIENTS

◇	1	chipotle pepper in adobo sauce
◇	1 teaspoon	adobo sauce
◇	1 teaspoon	lime juice
◇	1 cup	mayonnaise
◇	1 teaspoon	salt

1 Chop the pepper finely and place in a mixing bowl along with the adobo sauce, lime juice, mayonnaise, and salt. Stir to combine.

2 Serve on Fish Tacos. Store leftovers in an airtight container in refrigerator for up to 3 days.

SPARKLING MINT LEMONADE

PREP	COOK	MAKES
5	1	2
MINUTES	HOUR	QUARTS

INGREDIENTS

◇	1 quart	lemonade
◇	½ bunch	fresh mint leaves
◇	1 quart	sparkling water
◇		ice cubes
◇		

1 In a pitcher, combine the lemonade and fresh mint. Refrigerate for 1 hour.

2 Pour the sparkling water into the pitcher and stir to combine.

3 Serve in glasses with ice cubes.

SF

San Francisco Giants Baseball Club

AT&T PARK

LOCATION	San Francisco, California
OPENED	2000
CAPACITY	41,915
NICKNAMES	The Phone

In the spring of 2000, the San Francisco Giants opened their season in a new home. They moved from windy Candlestick Park, which they shared with the NFL's 49ers, to Pacific Bell Park. Later, AT&T bought the naming rights, and it is now known as AT&T Park. The Giants' new home has been good to both players and team alike. On August 7, 2007, slugger Barry Bonds belted his 756th home run to pass the great Hank Aaron as the all-time HR leader. A few years later, Matt Cain pitched a perfect game there on June 13, 2012. The team has also won three World Series titles (2010, 2012, and 2014) since the move.

CARIBBEAN RICE BOWL

with PINEAPPLE SALSA & CRANBERRY-GINGER FIZZ

AT&T Park sits on the edge of downtown San Francisco, along the water. Most seats curve around home plate and offer a spectacular view of San Francisco Bay. Being located in sunny California and near the water makes fruity drinks and seafood dishes a popular choice. But it's the Caribbean rice bowl, the Cha Cha Bowl, that is the fan favorite.

CARIBBEAN RICE BOWL

PREP	COOK	MAKES
10 MINUTES	25 MINUTES	4 BOWLS

INGREDIENTS

◇	1 cup	white rice
◇	1 tablespoon + 1 teaspoon	olive oil, divided
◇	2 cups	chicken broth
◇	1 teaspoon	crushed garlic
◇	1 teaspoon	turmeric
◇	1 pound	boneless chicken breasts
◇	1 teaspoon	cumin
◇	½ teaspoon	cayenne pepper
◇	½ teaspoon	allspice
◇	1 teaspoon	salt
◇	1 15-ounce can	black beans, drained
◇	8 ounces	frozen corn
◇	1	bell pepper
◇	1 recipe	pineapple salsa
◇	optional toppings: grated cheese, sour cream,	
◇	or guacamole (see page 65)	
◇		
◇		
◇		
◇		
◇		

1. In a saucepan, combine rice, 1 teaspoon olive oil, chicken broth, crushed garlic, and turmeric over medium heat. Bring to a simmer and cover. Cook for about 15 minutes or until the rice has absorbed all the liquid. Set aside.

2. Meanwhile, cut the chicken into bite-sized pieces and set aside.

3. In a mixing bowl, combine cumin, cayenne pepper, allspice, and salt. Add chicken and coat all sides.

4. In a skillet over medium-high heat, add 1 tablespoon olive oil. When the oil begins to smoke, carefully add the chicken and cook until no longer pink, about 10 minutes, stirring occasionally.

5. While the chicken cooks, heat the beans over low heat in a small saucepan.

6. Cook the corn according to package directions and set aside.

7. Chop the bell pepper into small pieces and set aside.

8. To assemble the bowl, place a heaping spoonful of rice in the bottom of the bowl. Add ¼ of the chicken, ¼ cup corn, ¼ cup beans, ¼ of the pepper, ¼ cup of pineapple salsa and desired garnishes. Serve hot.

PINEAPPLE SALSA

	PREP	COOK	MAKES
	15 MINUTES	**0** MINUTES	**1** CUP

	INGREDIENTS	
◇	½	pineapple
◇	1 recipe	pico de gallo (page 60)
◇	1 teaspoon	cumin
◇	1/8 teaspoon	cayenne pepper
◇	½ teaspoon	apple cider vinegar
◇	2 tablespoons	pineapple juice
◇		
◇		

1 Chop the pineapple into small pieces and add to mixing bowl.

2 Add pico de gallo, cumin, cayenne pepper, apple cider vinegar, and pineapple juice.

3 Stir well and serve on Caribbean Rice Bowl.

CRANBERRY-GINGER FIZZ

	PREP	COOK	MAKES
	5 MINUTES	**0** MINUTES	**2** QUARTS

	INGREDIENTS	
◇	1 quart	cranberry juice cocktail
◇	2 cups	ginger ale
◇	2 cups	lemonade
◇		ice cubes
◇		

1 In a pitcher, combine the cranberry juice, ginger ale, and lemonade. Stir well.

2 Serve in glasses with ice cubes.

About the Author

Katrina Jorgensen is a graduate of
Le Cordon Bleu College of Culinary Arts.
She enjoys creating new recipes and sharing
them with friends and family. She lives in
Rochester, Minnesota, with her husband,
Tony, and dog, Max.

Ballpark Cookbook The National League is published by
Capstone Press
1710 Roe Crest Drive, North Mankato, Minnesota 56003
www.mycapstone.com

Cataloging-in-Publication Data is available on the Library of Congress website.
ISBN: 978-1-4914-8233-9 (library hardcover)
ISBN: 978-1-4914-8623-8 (eBook PDF)

Contributing Writers: Blake A. Hoena and Donald Lemke
Editor: Donald Lemke
Designer: Bob Lentz
Art Director: Heather Kindseth
Media Researcher: Eric Gohl
Food Stylist: Sarah Schuette
Production Specialist: Tori Abraham

Photo Credits:
Dreamstime: Kmiragaya, 8; Eric Gohl: 48; Shutterstock: Aimee M Lee, 31 (chili), arigato, 51 (cutting board), bonchan, 19 (bottom left), Brenda Carson, 58 (groceries), Chiyacat, 34–35 (sausages), Coprid, 42 (cup), Dan Kosmayer, 47 (corn dog), Daniel M. Silva, 15 (bottom left), Foodio, 19 (bottom right), Jamie Cross, 47 (label), Julia Ivantsova, 1 (pencil), 64 (pencil), Linda Vostrovska, 6 (peach), littleny, 15 (bottom right), M. Unal Ozmen, 22–23 (fry boxes), Michael Dechev, 46 (keychain), Mike Flippo, cover (stadium), Moises Fernandez Acosta, cover (ketchup bottle), 39 (ketchup bottle), Picsfive, 14 (apple), 22 (French fry), pirtuss, 43 (ravioli), pukach, cover (French fries), Richard Peterson, 51 (oven mitt), Steve Broer, 24, Stuart Monk, 1 (chili dog), Tim UR, 6 (peach); Sports Illustrated: Al Tielemans, 12, Damian Strohmeyer, 16, David E. Klutho, 28, 36, 40, John Biever, 32, Peter Read Miller, 54 (bottom), Robert Beck, 44, 52, 56, 60, Simon Bruty, 4, 20

All recipe photographs by Capstone Studio: Karon Dubke.

All other images and design elements provided by Shutterstock.

Printed in Canada.
092015   009223FRS16